Carbon Trade: The Dawn of a New Age of Investing

An Introduction to Investing in a Sustainable World. Learn the Secrets to Profiting from the Most Valuable Ecological Asset: A Green Planet!

James Prosper

Carbon Trade: The Dawn of a New Age of Investing

Copyright © 2021

All rights reserved.

CONTENTS

    Preface   1

1. **Introduction to Carbon Trading**   3
   Background
   What is Carbon Credit?
   Climate Change
   The Cause of Climate Change
       Greenhouse Effect
       Greenhouse Gases and Human Intervention
       Carbon Trading as an Effective Instrument to Combat Climate Change
   Genesis of Carbon Markets
   Carbon as a New Commodity
   Carbon Trading Today and Tomorrow

2. **The History of the Carbon Trade**   13
   Introduction to the Kyoto Protocol
   "In a Nutshell"
   Annex I Parties
   Annex II Parties
   Annex B
   The Kyoto Mechanisms
   International Emissions Trading
   Clean Development Mechanism
   Joint Implementation
   Reserves vs. Overselling
   Monitoring Parties and Their Commitments
   Adapting to the Effects of Climate Change

3. **An Overview of the Top Carbon Markets Globally**   23
   Europe
   Carbon Markets in the United States
   China: The World's Biggest Carbon Market

4.	**How to Invest in Carbon Markets**	29
	Investing in Carbon	
	How is a Carbon Price Established?	
	How Does One Invest in Carbon Credits?	
	What are Carbon-Linked ETFs?	
	Why Do I Want to Invest?	
	Carbon Intensity ESG Scores	
	Investing in Carbon Capture Technologies	
	Further Discussion	
5.	**Future of Carbon Trade and the Challenges to Creating New Carbon Markets**	37
	Australia and the Politics of Climate Policy	
	America and Emissions Trading	
6.	**Alternative Ways to Invest in Carbon with Carbon-Backed Cryptocurrencies**	43
	Carbon Credits and Crypto	
	Early Projects	
	Elon Musk and the MicroStrategy-Tesla Bitcoin Bet	
7.	**Why Invest in Carbon**	49
	Profitability and Prospects	
	The Climate Pledge	
8.	**Tips to Investing in Carbon**	53
	Deciding Your Investment Goals	
	How Much You Want to Invest	
	How You Choose to Invest in Carbon	
	Selecting the Carbon Markets	
	Carbon Linked Funds	
	Advanced Due Diligence	
	Regulatory Compliance	
	Carbon-Backed Assets	
	Check Liquidity and Locking	

9. Why We Need Carbon Trade: Carbon Emission
   and its Impact on the Environment   57
The Conclusion: Pros and Cons of Investing in Carbon Markets   67
   Pros of Investing in Carbon Markets
      By Investing in Carbon, You Also Invest in the Future of the Planet
      Global Market
      One of the Most Profitable Asset Classes
      The Market Size
      Multiple Options to Invest in Carbon
      Carbon Neutrality is Corporate Goal of Industry Leaders

Carbon Trade: The Dawn of a New Age of Investing

PREFACE

Over the past decade and a half, carbon markets have emerged all across the globe. Recently, China, one of the biggest carbon-emitting nations on the planet, has also created the biggest carbon market in the world. As the focus shifts on combating climate change and cutting carbon emissions, the carbon trade is gaining popularity. Investing in carbon is undoubtedly a financially profitable venture. It's also a way to contribute to the sustainable future of the planet. It effectively helps offset carbon emissions.

In the coming years, the global carbon markets will double in size. As big multinational corporations and top economies are pledging carbon neutrality, the price of carbon will likely skyrocket. Reports suggest that by 2050, the carbon trade will be a $16 trillion market.

However, too many gaps in information about carbon markets have been a deterrent. This book can be your starting point to help you become an active player in the market. It details all you need to know about carbon markets and how to invest and profit from the carbon trade. It includes an in-depth analysis of carbon trade, the history of carbon pricing to understand the global carbon market structures, how they work, and why they work the way they do.

The goal is to empower the modern-day investor with real-time information and tips to succeed in this groundbreaking carbon trade world.

Sincerely,

James Prosper

CHAPTER 1

INTRODUCTION TO CARBON TRADING

Over the past two decades, carbon, as a commodity, an ecological asset, has been gaining popularity amongst investors. However, in the past four to five years, it has become increasingly popular. As global governments and international organizations continue to ramp up their efforts to combat climate change by actively taking measures to limit carbon emissions, carbon markets are growing and continue to offer both security and profits to investors. To many investors, including these ecological assets in their portfolio has helped them achieve investment goals. While the underlying ideas and concepts behind carbon trading are simple, it can be confusing for an average investor if one is not very familiar with the proceedings and how carbon markets work. In the first two chapters, we will take a deep dive and learn all about the concepts, the history, and the background of the carbon trade.

Background

To begin with, we must understand the background of modern carbon markets for better clarity. Earth's climate is getting warmer. The latest on record was one of the warmest. Since NASA (National Aeronautics and Space Administration) began recording global surface temperature in 1880, which was at -0.16 degrees Celsius, it has recently recorded the highest at 1.02 degrees Celsius for 2020 (tied with the record of the year 2016).

Humanity now faces global adversity that could change the fate of our planet and all that thrives on it. Climate change may already be at its worst state, but combating it with many solutions is our challenge. One of the straightforward solutions on the table is to manage and reduce greenhouse gases emissions. However, that's not easy, and it requires collaborative efforts from governments across the globe. Many countries have responded, initiated new climate actions, and have been continually innovating. How effective the measures taken by individual governments are, how fast we are acting to combat climate change is a different debate. In this book, we try to focus on what we have at hand and stick to facts to understand the carbon markets and their components.

What is Carbon Credit?

The single biggest ecological asset sold and traded in carbon markets is Carbon Credit. Here's a simplified flowchart to help you understand what Carbon Credits are.

Carbon Trade: The Dawn of a New Age of Investing

The emission of Carbon dioxide (CO2) and other greenhouse gases are disastrous to our environment.

↓

Factories and industries across the globe are one the biggest sources of these disastrous gases.

↓

The governments and global organizations have asked these "sources" to limit their emission of CO2 and other toxic gases.

↓

Now, these enterprises producing CO2 and other toxic gases have to limit their emissions and purchase a "Carbon Credit" to go beyond a certain limit.

↓

Carbon Credit is a permit that allows these companies and industries to emit a certain amount of carbon. It is a paid permit. With one Carbon Credit, the permit holder can emit one ton of CO2.

↓

Because Carbon Credits are costly, companies worldwide are trying to decrease their "toxic emissions." Studies reveal that the Carbon Credit system has been highly influential in limiting the emission of CO2 globally.

↓

However, companies can't bring their CO2 emission rates to zero. As such, many companies have to purchase Carbon Credit regularly.

↓

It has led to the creation of a global Carbon Credit market. The market is expanding, and as we get more and more focused on limiting global carbon emission, the market will expand.

Now, carbon markets and trading are gaining momentum worldwide and consequently pushing forward its potential in effectively reducing GHG emissions in the atmosphere. As an asset class, Carbon Credits have gained significantly in recent years. For example, the EU ETS Carbon Credit Futures has gained 574% in about two years. It has also beaten the most profitable stocks and the leading cryptocurrency Bitcoin in terms of profitability. As businesses and governments across the globe move to decarbonize the environment, the market is expected to grow at a breakneck pace. Research and data aggregator firms estimate that carbon will be a $16 trillion market if we get closer to achieving minimum carbon emissions. By pricing carbon, governments hope to put a full stop to the adverse effects of climate change.

Climate Change

It is crucial to understand climate change and government responses to understand how carbon markets are structured. Long-term change in the weather patterns (at the average) "that have come to define Earth's local, regional and global climates" is how our scientists at NASA define climate change.

Aside from the increasing global surface temperatures, warming oceans, decreasing ice sheets in Greenland and the Antarctic, retreating glaciers, decreasing spring snow cover in the Northern Hemisphere, rising global sea level, rapidly declining Arctic Sea ice, increasing acidity of surface ocean waters, increasing number of events related to record high or low temperatures, and heavy and sustained rainfalls all point to climate change.

With scientists predicting that the change in our little planet's climate will continue for the coming years and beyond, future effects of this climate change are expected.

One of the effects of climate change is the continued rising of global surface temperatures. Other foreseen effects of climate change include lengthening frost-free and growing seasons, increased precipitation patterns, intense droughts, heatwaves, stronger and more intense hurricanes, and increased flooding due to the rise of sea level with storm surges and high tides.

Scientists also predict that the Arctic Ocean would be ice-free before the middle of the century.

The Cause of Climate Change

To understand what is causing climate change and grasp how it could be remedied, we need to understand the elements or factors surrounding it – greenhouse effect, greenhouse gases, and human intervention.

Greenhouse Effect

Our planet has its way of warming its surface naturally. The greenhouse effect is the natural process where the Sun's energy that reaches the Earth is absorbed, trapped, and re-radiated by greenhouse gases. The absorbed and trapped energy warms the Earth's atmosphere and its surface.

However, not everything of the Sun's energy that enters the Earth's atmosphere is absorbed and trapped. Naturally, the amount absorbed and trapped is determined by how much greenhouse gases are present or concentrated in the atmosphere.

The greenhouse effect helps the Earth maintain a global surface temperature for life to survive or for this planet to become a comfortable place to live in. In the absence of this, the Sun's direct heat could fry every living organism on earth.

In other words, greenhouse gases are naturally produced and present in our atmosphere to serve as a glass blanket protecting us from too much heat from the Sun and warming our surface just enough for us to enjoy the day's weather.

Greenhouse Gases and Human Intervention

Greenhouse gases include water vapor (H_2O), carbon dioxide (CO_2), nitrous oxide (N_2O), methane (CH_4). These gases are naturally produced. Water vapor, for example, is naturally added to the atmosphere via evaporation. Carbon dioxide is released when plants and animals breathe. The natural decomposition of any organic material on earth produces methane. Volcanoes also release some of these greenhouse gases.

With just enough greenhouse gases in our atmosphere, there is nothing to worry about. However, as humans continue to explore and exploit the Earth's natural resources, more of these gases are released because of certain human activities.

Large quantities of carbon dioxide have been released into the atmosphere from burning fossil fuels, electric power plants, cars, trucks, airplanes, factories, mining, and deforestation.

After several years of natural gas processing and coal mining to produce fossil fuel, livestock farming, and mounting landfills, human beings added more methane to the atmosphere.

Agriculture and large mono-crop plantations contribute to more nitrous oxide in the atmosphere.

Refrigeration and cooling products manufacturers have also added fluorinated gases such as chlorofluorocarbons (CFCs), hydrochlorofluorocarbons (HCFCs), and hydrofluorocarbons (HFCs) to the earth's atmosphere.

Imagine all of these greenhouse gases already concentrated in the atmosphere along with the naturally produced ones - a thicker blanket that absorbs and traps more energy from the Sun.

The more energy absorbed in the atmosphere and the more energy trapped on the Earth's surface means warmer temperatures for the planet. Take note that even a slight global surface temperature change would have significant effects on the planet and every single living organism on it.

Thus, climate change. Just before we fully understood it, we are already facing the impact of climate change on a global scale: global warming.

The problem is now at hand. We look forward to the solution.

Carbon Trading as an Effective Instrument to Combat Climate Change

A straightforward solution to climate change was first presented and agreed upon by the parties to the 1994 United Nations Framework Convention on Climate Change (UNFCCC) - to manage and reduce GHG emissions to the atmosphere. And in 1997, the Kyoto Protocol to the UNFCCC laid down the mechanisms to these solutions adopted by 192 countries.

The solution's framework is for industrialized countries and economies in transition to commit to taking the principal obligation of reducing GHG emissions to the atmosphere. This framework is based on the fact that these countries were noted as the major contributors to GHG emissions.

Even as the principle of reducing GHG emission rests on respective countries' national measures and capabilities, the Kyoto Protocol also designed and introduced market-based mechanisms to aid these countries in meeting the targets assigned to them.

United Nations Framework Convention on Climate Change

Genesis of Carbon Markets

These mechanisms that the Kyoto Protocol introduced were flexible and have already gone far from where it first took off.

Nevertheless, it's worth taking the time to look back at how the Carbon Market debuted in the trading world.

There were three flexible market-based mechanisms to begin with. The first is the International Emissions Trading mechanism, the second is the Clean Development Mechanism or CDM, and the last is the Joint Implementation mechanism.

The core principle of these three mechanisms is to help the main complaint to the GHG emission reduction target achieve the goal by implementing measures where it's going to be economical.

This means that these mechanisms help reduce GHG emissions regardless of where a corresponding project or activity is implemented, and as insinuated, be it in a developing country.

To stress the point, what is vital for these mechanisms is that GHGs are removed or reduced from our atmosphere.

A grasp of these principles will encourage first-world countries and the private sector to invest in "green" projects or activities that do not use old and harmful technologies that modern but clean systems and infrastructures can very well replace. Moreover, it is perceived that these projects are even more cost-efficient and may offer longer-term benefits.

Carbon as a New Commodity

GHG emissions, subsequently, became a commodity as initiated by the International emissions trading mechanism. Trading of GHG emissions allowed participating countries to trade or sell extra units of emissions that are over their assigned target to other countries that would need more these units

This gave birth to a new commodity - emissions reduction or removal units. However, carbon dioxide is the main greenhouse constituent. It has become convenient for transactions to ascribe these units or credits as carbon units or Carbon Credits.

So people became accustomed to talking of carbon trading instead of emission reductions or removals.

As it is now, carbon is already tracked and traded, as would any other commodity present in the market. And a new market is created as well - the carbon market.

The two other Kyoto mechanisms allowed the emissions trading to flourish. The Clean Development Mechanism, for example, encourages parties to the Protocol to implement emission-removal activities in the developing countries as hosts of CDM projects.

A host country to a CDM will earn certified emission reduction credits or CERs equivalent to one tonne of CO_2. These CERs can be traded to developed countries for them to meet part of their emission reduction targets.

This trading mechanism has allowed countries to offset the required emission reduction target they cannot, for the moment, avoid. They are allowed to do this by investing in projects somewhere else that will contribute to the reduction of emissions of GHGs.

The Joint Implementation mechanism carries the same principle in play. Only the compliant country to an assigned emission reduction target can earn ERUs or emission reduction units by implementing a GHG emission reduction or removal project in another partner country.

This mechanism offers benefits to both the developed country and the developing country. The former can meet a part of its emission reduction target economically, and the latter gains from technology transfer and investment from the former.

From these emissions trading schemes, the carbon market and carbon trading are also revolving. These schemes had provided countries a way to meet their targets and help developing countries simultaneously.

From these schemes, the following units or credits were created to be the basis of emissions trading and later on with carbon trading: RMU or removal unit - a unit based activities related to land use, land-use change, and forestry such as reforestation; ERU or Emission reduction unit - a unit generated by a joint implementation project; and CER or Certified emission reduction - a unit generated from a CDM activity.

Carbon Trading Today and Tomorrow

With all of these mechanisms promoting ways to manage, reduce or remove GHG emissions from the atmosphere and offering ways to help developing countries participate in this endeavor, the carbon market and its trading activities are going to hit the HOT charts.

Not to mention that the Carbon Market has made tremendous strides from where it made its first steps in just a short period. But that's the motivating aspect only. The best part is the actual impact the carbon trading already has.

Regardless of the motive each participant has in the carbon trade, be it economical or purely environmental, the impact we're taking into account is the amount of GHGs removed from our planet's atmosphere.

This is not to say that other efforts are useless. But for the world to have found a way to motivate a concerted climate action that encourages first-world countries to partner with the developing world to solve the problem posed by climate change is a milestone the Earth deserves.

The battle is long and far from over. But with more countries embracing the principles of the carbon market, initiating and innovating on the carbon trade mechanism, it is more than convincing that among all other efforts, Carbon Trading is so far the world's effective instrument to combat climate change.

Carbon Trade: The Dawn of a New Age of Investing

CHAPTER 2

THE HISTORY OF THE CARBON TRADE

To understand how carbon markets evolved and how they operate, it is essential to learn about the history of the Carbon Trade. Putting a price on carbon and charging businesses and restricting countries from emitting more toxic gases into the environment stem from the Kyoto Protocol. You must have heard about the Kyoto Protocol, which is often connected with climate change, global warming, and carbon trade. In this chapter, as we explore the history and how carbon markets came into existence, we will learn in-depth about the Kyoto Protocol. It will help us understand the fundamentals of carbon markets and how they are structured, and why they are structured the way they are.

Introduction to the Kyoto Protocol

The Kyoto Protocol is an international agreement that embodies diplomatic rules and mechanisms to limit and reduce greenhouse gases (GHG) emissions.

GHGs are atmospheric gases found to be the cause of global warming and climate change as they absorb and re-emit infrared radiation. Carbon dioxide (CO_2), methane (CH_4), and nitrous oxide (N_2O) are the major GHGs found in the atmosphere now.

The United Nations drafted The Kyoto Protocol following the United Nations Framework Convention on Climate Change (UNFCCC) in March 1994 and ratified by 197 countries known as the Parties of the Convention.

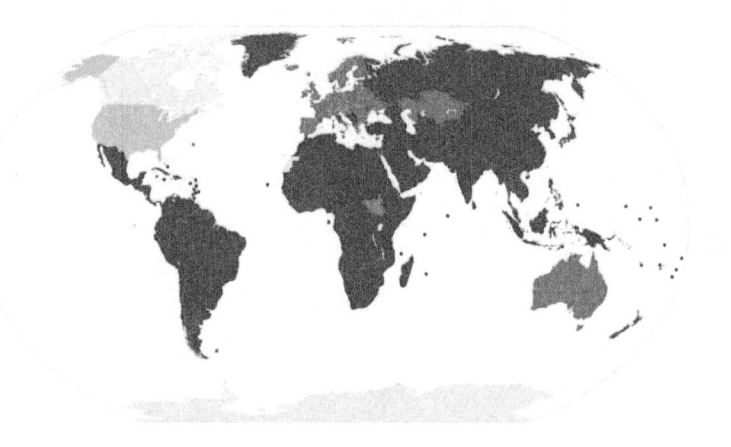

The protocol was adopted on December 11, 1997, but came into force on February 16, 2005. One hundred and ninety-two parties conferred and signed the agreement.

The UNFCCC laid down its ultimate goal to "prevent 'dangerous' human interference with the climate system."

The protocol operationalizes this by gathering commitments from industrialized countries and economies in transition (EIT) according to their agreed respective individual targets.

The convention can only ask for these countries to espouse these principles. Whereas, the protocol has made parties commit to adopting policies and measures agreed to lessen the gravity of the problem posed by climate change vis-a-vis GHG emissions.

In a Nutshell

"The Kyoto Protocol is a United Nations international agreement adopted by 192 parties in 1997 under the 1994 United Nations Framework Convention on Climate Change. The protocol operationalizes the Convention's adopted policies and measures to mitigate the problems posed by climate change and GHG emissions."

"Common but differentiated responsibility and respective capabilities."

Guided by this idea, The Kyoto Protocol only binds developed countries as the agreement itself is based on the principles and provisions of the UNFCCC, which follows an annex-based structure.

In other words, The Kyoto Protocol and the UNFCCC put a heavier burden on these countries in recognition of them being primarily responsible for the currently high atmospheric levels of GHG emissions.

Annex I Parties

Annex I to the UNFCCC is the list of industrialized countries committed to managing and reducing their greenhouse emissions to the 1990 levels by 2000.

These countries have also agreed to the emission targets for the period of 2008 to 2012.

The list includes the twenty-four original members of the OECD or the Organization for Economic Co-operation and Development, the European Union, the 14 countries with economies in transition.

Table of Countries Listed under Annex I to the United Nations Framework Convention on Climate Change			
Australia	Estonia	Liechtenstein	Russian Federation
Austria	Finland	Lithuania	Slovakia
Belarus	France	Luxembourg	Slovenia
Belgium	Germany	Malta	Spain
Bulgaria	Greece	Monaco	Sweden
Canada	Hungary	Netherlands	Switzerland
Croatia	Iceland	New Zealand	Turkey
Cyprus	Ireland	Norway	Ukraine
Czech Republic	Italy	Poland	UK and Northern Ireland
Denmark	Japan	Portugal	
European Economic Community	Latvia	Romania	United States of America

Annex II Parties

Annex II to the UNFCCC has listed countries endowed with the special obligation to provide financial resources and technology transfer to developing countries. Included in the list are the original members of the OECD and the European Union.

Having identified these countries by the UNFCCC, the Kyoto Protocol has set binding targets of emission reduction in industrialized countries, EITs, and the EU (Annex B to the Kyoto Protocol).

Annex B

Annex B to the Kyoto Protocol. Table of Countries/Parties with Targets of Quantified Emission Limitation or Reduction Commitment (Percentage of Base Year or Period)					
Country	Target	Country	Target	Country	Target
Australia	108	Greece	92	Norway	101
Austria	92	Hungary	94	Poland	94
Belgium	92	Iceland	110	Portugal	92
Bulgaria	92	Ireland	92	Romania	92
Canada	94	Italy	92	Russian Federation	100
Croatia	95	Japan	94	Slovakia	92
Czech Republic	92	Latvia	92	Slovenia	92
Denmark	92	Liechtenstein	92	Spain	92
Estonia	92	Lithuania	92	Sweden	92
European Community	92	Luxembourg	92	Switzerland	92
Finland	92	Monaco	92	Ukraine	100
France	92	Netherlands	92	UK and Northern Ireland	92
Germany	92	New Zealand	100	USA	93

These targets altogether sum up to a five percent emission reduction compared to the levels in the year 1990 for the first five-year commitment period (2008-2012).

An amendment to the Kyoto Protocol in December 2012 was adopted in Doha, Qatar, which outlines a second commitment period from 2013 to 2020: the DOHA Amendment.

The new amendment to the Kyoto Protocol has yet to enter into force, which needs a total of 144 instruments of acceptance. The composition of parties is different from the first period of commitment.

Regardless, it is still important to understand how the Kyoto Protocol to the UNFCCC is helping manage GHG emissions and combat global warming and climate change.

The Kyoto Mechanisms

The Kyoto Protocol has established essential mechanisms to help countries achieve their targets. According to the protocol, parties are required to meet their targets via national means, principally.

The Kyoto Protocol, however, has established flexible market mechanisms that will help countries meet these targets. These mechanisms are based on the trade of emissions permits.

These mechanisms propose that targets may also be achieved using these three market-based mechanisms, namely (a) the International Emissions Trading; (b) Clean Development Mechanism or CDM; and lastly (c) Joint Implementation or JI.

The protocol has outlined these mechanisms to preferably encourage GHG management and reduction to be implemented where it's cost-efficient.

As an example, the Kyoto Protocol suggests that these mechanisms can be implemented in the developing world. These mechanisms put forward the idea that emissions will be reduced. As long as the emissions are removed from the atmosphere, they should not be of great concern.

The same benefits are expected of encouraging green investments in said developing countries. The private sector must also be included in this endeavor to minimize and hold steady GHG emissions at a safe level.

This way, the possibility of discarding the use of older, harmful technology and newer, cleaner infrastructure and systems becomes more cost-effective. Longer-term benefits are likewise expected.

It is important for Annex I Parties under the UNFCCC to provide information in their national communications under the Kyoto Protocol.

This information must demonstrate that implementing these additional mechanisms is supplemental to their domestic climate action to meet their targets.

The Compliance Committee is tasked to assess this information.

International Emissions Trading

International Emissions Trading is one of the flexible mechanisms the Kyoto Protocol has set out to help Annex B countries meet targets.

This mechanism views GHG emission as a new commodity, thus, emissions trading.

As laid down by the Kyoto Protocol, emissions trading permits countries with spare emission units (emissions that are permitted but not used) to trade or sell these extra units to countries over their targets.

This mechanism has facilitated the creation of a new commodity: emission reductions or removals. Carbon dioxide being the principal greenhouse gas, has now become a means to communicate when trading emissions. People simply speak about carbon trading when trading emission reductions.

Now, carbon is tracked and traded like any other commodity in the market. This has now been referred to as the "carbon market."

Clean Development Mechanism

The Clean Development Mechanism or CDM is a market-based mechanism. The Kyoto Protocol considers one of the flexible ways to help manage GHG emissions and help industrialized countries meet their targets and commitment to the UNFCCC.

The CDM promotes and allows the implementation of emission-reduction projects in developing countries to earn certified emission reduction credits or CER credits.

Each CER credit is equivalent to one tonne of CO_2. CERs are designed to be traded and sold to industrialized countries for them to meet a part of their target emission reduction as agreed under the Kyoto Protocol.

This mechanism is expected to stimulate sustainable development and reduction in GHG emissions. At the same time, giving them the flexibility in implementing means to meet their limitation target or emission reduction targets.

This offsetting is considered a climate action enabling individuals and organizations alike to make up for the emission they can't yet avoid by investing and supporting recognized projects that aim to reduce emissions elsewhere.

Joint Implementation

The Kyoto Protocol, through the Joint Implementation mechanism, also allows a country with a commitment to emission reduction or limitation to earn emission reduction units (ERU) from a project in another country (Annex B).

This project has to be an emission-reduction or emission removal project. Each ERU is equivalent to one tonne of CO_2. Therefore, this ERU can be counted toward meeting its Kyoto target.

The Joint Implementation mechanism offers parties a flexible and cost-effective way of meeting a portion of their Kyoto commitments. Consequently, the host Party of the project also benefits from investment and technology transfer from the said Party.

Under the Kyoto Protocol, the emissions trading scheme comes with more than actual emission units traded and sold.

Each of the following units, which may be traded under the scheme, is equivalent to one tonne of CO_2:

1. **Removal Unit (RMU):** based on land use, land-use change, and forestry (LULUCCF) activities such as reforestation
2. **Emission Reduction Unit (ERU):** generated by a joint implementation project
3. **Certified Emission Reduction (CER):** generated from a CDM project activity

Reserves vs. Overselling

There is a concern about parties "overselling" units. To address this concern, and perhaps in the future, if they cannot meet their Kyoto commitment or their own emissions targets, the Kyoto Protocol requires each Party to maintain a reserve of ERUs, CERs, and/or RMUs in its national registry.

Known as the "commitment period reserve," each Party's reserve should not exceed 90% of its assigned amount. Or each Party's reserve should be 100% of "five times its most recently reviewed inventory, whichever is lowest."

Transactions involving these units, such as transfers and acquisitions, are tracked and monitored. This is done via the Registry Systems under the Kyoto Protocol.

To ensure the security of transfers of emission between any of these units between two countries, the Kyoto Protocol has an International transaction log.

Monitoring Parties and Their Commitments

The protocol also made sure to set up a rigorous monitoring, review, and verification mechanism. It serves as a compliance monitor that ensures transparency. It holds parties accountable and responsible for their commitments to the protocol.

Under the protocol and as agreed by parties, countries' actual emissions have to be monitored. In addition, trades carried out must be precisely recorded.

The Kyoto Protocol handles monitoring via its Registry Systems, which track and record all Parties' transactions in implementing the mechanisms.

An International transaction log is maintained to verify the consistency of transactions with the Kyoto Protocol. The UN Climate Change Secretariat keeps this log in Bonn, Germany, where it is based.

Parties must also accomplish reporting by submitting emission inventories annually and national reports under the protocol at regular intervals.

The Kyoto Protocol has established a compliance system to ensure that all parties are on track to meet their commitments. This way, the protocol can help parties meet their commitments if problems arise in doing so.

Adapting to the Effects of Climate Change

Like its precursor, the UNFCCC, the Kyoto Protocol is designed and outlined to help countries adapt to the harmful effects of climate change.

As such, it assists in developing and deploying technologies geared toward increasing the resilience of countries to the impacts of climate change.

An Adaption Fund was established for this purpose. The fund will finance projects and programs in developing countries or parties to the Kyoto Protocol.

This fund was mainly financed in the first commitment period with a share of proceeds from activities of the CDM project.

In the DOHA Amendment, a 2% share of proceeds from international emissions trading and joint implementation was decided to provide the Adaptation Fund for the second commitment period.

CHAPTER 3

AN OVERVIEW OF THE TOP CARBON MARKETS GLOBALLY

Once the majority of the countries signed the Kyoto Protocol, carbon emission was to come at a price for factories and industries pumping toxic emissions into the environment. And Carbon Credits which allowed these companies to emit one tonne of Carbon Dioxide (CO_2) into the atmosphere, gradually became an asset with a value. As a result, several countries developed their carbon trading systems.

The European Union Emissions Trading System (EU ETS) was the first major greenhouse gas emissions trading system. Since its launch in 2005, other major economies have launched similar Carbon Credit programs, including China and the US, which are currently the world's two largest polluting nations. They contribute 27% and 15% to global emissions, compared to the EU's 10%. Unlike China and the EU, the US doesn't have an emissions trading system spanning its entirety. The US lacks a national carbon market. Instead, states interested in an emissions trading system have to decide individually whether to make their cap-and-trade system like California or join the Regional Greenhouse Gas Initiative, which has eleven participating states, including New York and Massachusetts.

Europe

The European Union Emissions Trading System was surrounded by doubts about its effectiveness in its early years for various reasons, from oversupplies of Carbon Credits to windfall profits. Still, since then, it's been shown to be a valuable tool for reducing carbon emissions. Within the EU ETS, Carbon Credits are called EU Allowances (EUA). EUAs are among the highest-priced Carbon Credits in the world due to the scope of the EU ETS and the consistently decreasing supply of EUAs.

The EU ETS was designed to operate in several phases, with the system expanding over time and having a greater role in reducing emissions in the EU. The first phase ran from 2005 to 2007, and in this phase, the ETS had a low reduction goal: lower emissions by 1-2% across the EU. It failed in that task, partly due to the difficulty of forecasting emissions. The second phase (2008 - 2012) greatly expanded the ETS and included three non-EU members: Norway, Iceland, and Liechtenstein. Toward the end of the second phase, aviation emissions were included in the ETS, causing significant pushback from other nations, including the US, China, India, and Russia, so not all flights are covered by the ETS—only flights within the European Economic Area are.

One of the ETS's major criticisms was that it provided windfall profits to polluting firms because EUAs were allocated at first. A response to this criticism came in the third phase (2013 - 2020), where there was an auctioning process for EUAs. In 2013, the percentage of Carbon Credits that were auctioned instead of allocated was 40%. Furthermore, an overall EU cap was set, and more sectors were included in the ETS.

The ETS entered its fourth phase in 2021, and the EU plans to reduce the supply of Carbon Credits by 2.2% every year in this phase, compared to 1.74% in the third phase. Furthermore, in the fourth phase, the market stability reserve, the ETS' mechanism to avoid a build-up of excess permits, will be strengthened. One thing is clear from these changes in the ETS over time: the EU carbon market has improved over time in response to valid criticism. Many of the lessons from the EU's carbon market have been absorbed by nations elsewhere—the most obvious and yet most important lesson being, of course, that carbon markets work.

Carbon Markets in the United States

In the US, RGGI (pronounced 'Reggie') was the first carbon market similar to the EU ETS. It was launched in 2009, though initial plans began six years prior with talks between governors of states. Seven states signed on at RGGI's beginning, although four more states have joined since then, and the membership of a twelfth state is pending (Pennsylvania). Over 90% of RGGI allowances are distributed through quarterly auctions, the proceeds from which states have put into programs ranging from clean energy to energy efficiency. RGGI has mechanisms to avoid having the price of Carbon Credits move above or below a specified range. They are aptly named the cost containment reserve (preventing businesses costs from rising too much) and the emissions containment reserve (preventing the cost for polluting from falling too much). In 2021, that range is $6 to $13, with upper and lower bounds of the range set to increase by 7% every following year.

One of the most successful aspects of RGGI has been its usefulness in reducing greenhouse gas emissions while its member states still experienced economic growth, showing that it's certainly possible to pursue economic and environmental goals at the same time. A 2011 independent report from the Analysis Group found that RGGI has a net positive economic impact on its member states, largely thanks to the proceeds from Carbon Credit auctions being put to use by state governments.

Meanwhile, on the West Coast, California also has a thriving carbon market. A cornerstone of the state's effort to reduce its carbon emissions has been its cap-and-trade program launched in 2013. The carbon market covers all sectors of California's economy and is among the largest carbon markets in the world. Proceeds from auctioning Carbon Credits have historically been a major source of revenue for the state, generating hundreds of millions of dollars per auction that the state has spent on various climate projects, including high-speed rail. Unfortunately, the economic trouble from COVID-19 resulted in the May 2020 auction bringing in merely $25 million for the state. Still, with the US economic recovery, the Californian carbon market has been returning to normal. Nevertheless, the program has been criticized for not inducing enough emissions reductions to help California meet its goal of a 40% emissions reduction relative to 1990 levels by 2030. ProPublica found that between 2013 and 2019, the carbon emissions from the state's oil and gas industry rose 3.5%.

California may offer a cautionary tale for states and nations seeking to use cap-and-trade to reduce carbon emissions. A carbon market is only effective with proper implementation and design. California may have set its early caps too high, creating an oversupply of Carbon Credits that companies could use far in the future when their price rises. The state has likely been too generous in giving free allowances to certain industries, like oil and gas drilling. Furthermore, California allows companies to purchase offsets to cancel out some of their emissions. However, various studies have raised serious doubts about the effectiveness of offset programs, including one study specifically about California's offset program: *Managing Uncertainty in Carbon Offsets*, which was written by researchers from the University of California, Berkeley, Stanford, and various other highly regarded institutions. The study found that the inclusion of offsets in the cap-and-trade system might indirectly end up helping coal mines last longer and inadvertently boost California's total level of pollution.

China: The World's Biggest Carbon Market

China is the newest of the world's three major polluters to create a carbon market. Suppose the Carbon Credit system is implemented well. In that case, it could have a significant effect on global carbon emissions since China alone is responsible for over a fourth of the world's CO_2 emissions. Even in its initial phase, covering less than half of China's emissions, the Chinese carbon market will be the world's largest, covering 12% of global carbon emissions. However, it remains to be seen how much more expansive the system will become and how willing Chinese officials are to trade off potential short-term economic gains for environmental benefits.

China's emissions trading scheme took nearly a decade of preparation. However, it's still experiencing a delay in its launch this year, and trading has yet to begin, despite reports from The Economist and TechCrunch that it began trading in February. Shanghai emissions contracts are set to begin trading in July, with power plants and electricity generators being the main participants in the carbon trading system. In addition, China has yet to provide a schedule for the reach of the emissions trading scheme. Still, it has announced plans to reduce its carbon intensity of GDP by 65% by 2030 relative to 2005 levels (carbon intensity of GDP is how much CO_2 is produced per dollar of GDP in the economy). Furthermore, China pledged late last year to become carbon neutral by 2060. As a result, its leadership seems to have high expectations for the trading system, believing it will achieve the goal of peaking Chinese CO_2 in 2030, a necessary milestone to reach its carbon neutrality target.

Carbon markets seem here to stay as a powerful tool for reducing carbon emissions. But the effectiveness of cap-and-trade programs in reducing emissions is highly dependent on the details of how those programs are implemented. Different programs in the same country can have vastly different results, like RGGI and California's cap-and-trade program. It remains to be seen how effective China's carbon market will be, but if it can achieve a similar level of success as the EU ETS and RGGI, the world could take a major step toward combating climate change.

CHAPTER 4

HOW TO INVEST IN CARBON MARKETS

Around the globe, people have gained awareness about the dangers of climate change and its causes. In response, governments have implemented several ways of reducing their carbon emissions. As you already know, one of those methods is emissions trading, often called cap-and-trade. A government distributes or sells permits to emit a specific amount of CO_2 (typically one ton for one Carbon Credit). Those permits end up on a free market where companies can buy or sell them from each other. The point of cap-and-trade is to put a price on carbon emissions and limit (or cap) their total amount within a country or region. The effect of putting them on the market is that when they're scarce or demand is too high, their price rises, encouraging companies to seek alternative energy sources.

You have also learned that the most prominent carbon market in the world is the EU. It created the European Union Emissions Trading System (EU ETS) in 2005 as a major component of its energy policy, making it the first major greenhouse gas emissions trading system globally. The EU ETS remains the largest system of its kind today. The system has not been free from hiccups: in 2007, its cap on emissions was too high and drove down the carbon price to zero—an issue stemming from the difficulty of forecasting emissions and the initially modest 1-2% emissions reduction that the EU sought. For years, it was seen as a failure in reducing emissions within and without the EU, but the system recently proved effective. A 2020 study found that the EU ETS has reduced the EU's carbon emissions by 3.8% between 2008 and 2016.

A newer carbon market was established in 2009 in the US, where eleven states are part of the Regional Greenhouse Gas Initiative (RGGI), a CO_2 cap-and-trade program. A twelfth state, Pennsylvania, is pending RGGI membership. In addition, the state of California has a cap-and-trade program. On a larger scale, the Commodities Futures Trading Commission recommended in September 2020 that Congress establish a method for carbon pricing to discourage polluters.

China launched a national carbon trading market in February 2021, but it has yet to be seen whether it's a serious effort to reduce carbon emissions. The government will initially allocate emissions allowances for free and later auction allowances "at the appropriate time according to the situation." Furthermore, China's state-owned enterprises and financial services firms have raised concerns about the carbon market's potentially harmful effect on profitability and lending risk.

Investing in Carbon

Carbon has conquered global trading and market since it has been assigned a value in international emissions trading. Carbon's value is founded on reducing or removing greenhouse gas emissions in the atmosphere and carbon dioxide being the major substance responsible for climate change.

As a new commodity, carbon now has a cost. This cost is ascribed to the pollution or damage greenhouse gases emissions from human activities have been causing.

Economists claim that this move has given a new motivation for an effective way to reduce GHG emissions worldwide.

How is a Carbon Price Established?

Since the time carbon was introduced as a commodity and international emissions trading took off, there are now two main ways to determine the price of carbon.

The first one is called the carbon tax. Governments impose it on any entity engaging in the distribution and sale of fossil fuels. The amount is calculated according to the carbon content found in fossil fuels.

The effect is somewhat predictable but tolerated. The increased cost of fuels and the goods and services dependent on them is intended to encourage businesses and individuals to consider and patronize less carbon-intensive production and consumption.

The second way is called the cap-and-trade model. It's a quota system where a particular country, region, or company are assigned total allowable emissions in advance, thus "capped." This quota for allowable emissions is expressed in "permits" to pollute. These permits are either auctioned or allocated to companies.

Then, these companies can trade these permits between one another, creating a carbon market.

How Does One Invest in Carbon Credits?

Investors of all shapes and sizes are now making more money investing in Carbon Credits. There are many ways to earn Carbon Credits. Carbon Credits are earned from a project or anything that has value in helping manage, reduce or remove GHGs from the atmosphere. Local governments award credit certificates for greener initiatives. These credits can then be sold to the carbon market. As an investor, you would focus on Carbon Credits.

Carbon Credits are valuable for companies who want to offset their emissions reduction targets. The potential in the carbon market is limitless. You can earn and sell as many credits as you want. One of the easiest ways to invest money in Carbon is to invest in carbon-linked exchange-traded funds.

What are Carbon-Linked ETFs?

Exchange-traded funds, to begin with, are like mutual funds - pooled money from different investors, each assigned a corresponding "share" equivalent to their stake in the sum of their money.

ETFs differ where their name suggests. It's exchange traded. As mutual funds are, ETFs also offer exposure to a specific area of the market. With an ETF, you can buy and/or stocks and shares in the market.

Unlike mutual funds, though, ETFs can be bought or sold anytime and anywhere. Therefore making it a lot more flexible, accessible, affordable to the public.

As such, ETFs can offer genuine and low-cost public access to practically any portfolio in the market today.

In other words, with an ETF, investors, big and small, are given access to the entire market from the US retail stocks, UK bonds, or Asian technology portfolio, and many more at an affordable price.

That explained, even carbon-linked ETFs are accessible for public trade.

We will be sharing a short list of carbon-linked ETFs you might want to consider investing in for this article only.

Why do I Want to Invest?

Carbon Allowances allow companies to receive economic incentives for achieving their emissions reduction targets or credits to offset their targets.

Here are two popular Carbon Intensive ETFs:

Symbol	ETF Name	Natural Resource	Total Assets ($MM)
KRBN	KraneShares Global Carbon ETF	Energy	$513.51
GRN	iPath Series B Carbon ETN	Energy	$55.30

Assets and Average Volume as of 2021-07-22 16:24 EDT

We can Evaluate Carbon Intensive ETFs via their Weighted Average Carbon Intensity across one metric ton and display tons of CO2 emission/$M sales.

The value will serve as a gauge of a certain fund's exposure to carbon-intensive companies.

The Weight Average Carbon Intensity score is the total of the ETF holding weight and is multiplied by the ETF holding Carbon Intensity.

Carbon Intensity ESG Scores

Symbol	ETF Name	Weighted Average Carbon Intensity (Tons of CO2e/$M Sales)
JPMB	JPMorgan USD Emerging Markets Sovereign Bond ETF	3372.93
CHIU	Global X MSCI China Utilities ETF	3225.13
JHMU	John Hancock Multifactor Utilities ETF	2640.43
XLU	Utilities Select Sector SPDR Fund	2555.7
RYU	Invesco S&P 500® Equal Weight Utilities ETF	2528.74

As of June 1, 2021. Lifted from ETF Database

VanEck Vectors Low Carbon Energy ETF (SMOG) and the iShares MSCI ACWI Low Carbon Target ETF (CRBN) are amongst other popular ETFs to invest in carbon. These ETFs are some top examples from the US. However, you can explore other such funds.

Investing in Carbon Capture Technologies

You may still find another way of investing your money into green projects or carbon capture ETFs. Have you heard of these companies: Net Power, Quest, Carbon Engineering, Global Thermostat, Climeworks, and Carbfix?

These companies were listed by The Green Market Oracle as the Top 6 best companies for carbon capture.

Companies engaged in carbon capture and storage technologies and processes aim to filter off excess carbon dioxide from the atmosphere. As a raw material, reuse carbon for some other use such as fuel, protein, etc.

Worthy of note is that around 1,000 billion tons of carbon dioxide from the atmosphere needed to be drawn down to prevent a global catastrophe in the future, already showing initial effects today via climate change and global warming.

Other companies to look forward to in 2021, according to Greenbiz, are Blue Planet, CCm Technologies, Carbon Upcycling Technologies, DyeCoo, and Kiverdi.

Other companies and organizations are also gearing to launch their versions of carbon capture and storage projects and technologies. So there is a lot to watch out for in the next couple of years.

Further Discussion

In September 2019, the information services firm IHS Markit launched the IHS Markit Global Carbon Index, a benchmark for the global price of Carbon Credits. The index currently covers the cost of Carbon Credits from the EU ETS, RGGI, and California's cap-and-trade program. In addition, the index allowed for the creation of the KraneShares Global Carbon ETF (KRBN), an exchange-traded fund benchmarked to the IHS Markit Global Carbon Index. This is one of the best ways investors can gain exposure to the carbon markets. The fund opened on July 30 at $20 a share and has risen to around $35 since then.

Another way to gain exposure to carbon markets is with the iPath Series B Carbon ETN, an exchange-traded note on the NYSE Arca. ETNs are debt securities that track an index and trade on an exchange like a typical stock. They do not provide ownership of stocks or other securities and are essentially a promise by the issuer that investors will be paid the return the tracked index produces. The iPath Series B Carbon ETN is issued by the British banking giant Barclays and tracks the Barclays Global Carbon II Index—the current components of that index are futures contracts trading on the ICE Futures Europe exchange. The index is heavily weighted toward the EU's Carbon Credits.

Given the goal of nations worldwide to reduce carbon emissions and avoid catastrophic climate change, systems like cap-and-trade are necessary to reign in polluting corporations. The advent of Carbon Credit indices and the investment vehicles that track them, like the KraneShares Global Carbon ETF, now allow investors to profit from this trend of rising carbon costs. The ideal model of green investing is to help the environment and earn a profit simultaneously and investing in Carbon Credits may be one of the best ways. The price of Carbon Credits is currently far lower than the estimates made by the values that leading economists say are necessary for the world to hit its temperature goals. So it's feasible that countries will continue to reduce the supplies of Carbon Credits over the next few years and hence raise their price.

Carbon Trade: The Dawn of a New Age of Investing

CHAPTER 5

FUTURE OF CARBON TRADE AND THE CHALLENGES TO CREATING NEW CARBON MARKETS

The European Union Emissions Trading System is the success story that nations from other areas can look to for an example of establishing and running similar systems of their own. Lessons from the EU ETS, such as auctioning credits instead of giving them out, have already been adopted in the Californian cap-and-trade system, the Regional Greenhouse Gas Initiative, and other emissions trading systems. The future of carbon markets seems bright: the Institute of International Finance predicts that the Carbon Credit market could be worth up to US$100 billion per year by 2050, the year that many countries around the world have set as their target for carbon neutrality. But there have been prominent carbon markets that have shut down, such as the Australian cap-and-trade system. Furthermore, while the US has two carbon markets on the state and regional levels, there isn't a national emissions trading system. And to understand the future of carbon markets, we should look to the past to see what's gone wrong and why some nations have been reluctant to implement one.

Australia and the Politics of Climate Policy

The Australian carbon markets had a rough start. The first iteration was the Carbon Pollution Reduction Scheme (CPRS), whose planning started in 2007 while the center-left Labor Party was in Opposition. The Labor Party won the 2007 federal election and formed a government, and in the next year, the Rudd government published its white paper on the CPRS. However, its legislation failed to pass due to opposition from the Liberal Party and the Greens, the third-largest Australian political party. As a result, the CPRS was scrapped, causing a significant loss of voters for the Labor Party. In the place of the CPRS, the Carbon Pricing Mechanism was included in the Clean Energy Act 2011, which successfully passed in February 2011 and took effect in 2012.

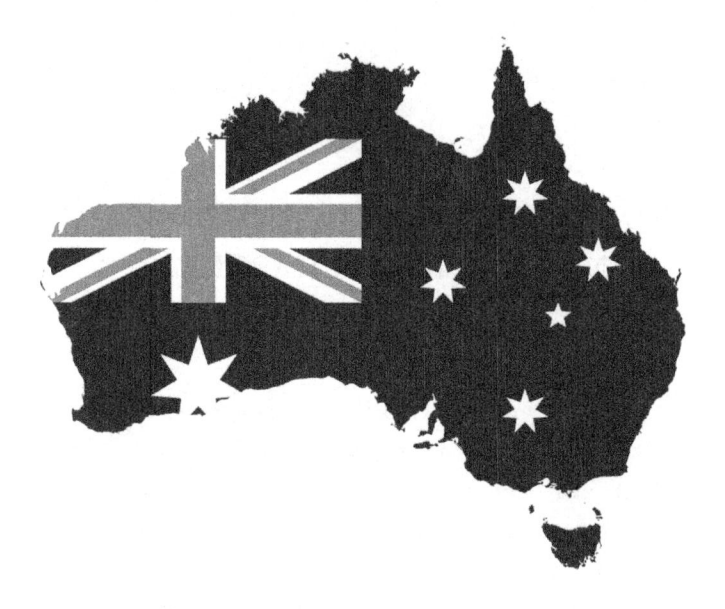

The Labor Party's attempts to implement a carbon pricing scheme failed to diminish new investment in the coal industry, which saw a 62% increase in spending on exploration between 2010 and 2011. When the Australian emissions trading system finally took effect, it was clear that its implementation was flawed. Only a few large electricity generators and larger industrial plants were included in the scheme. Australia's total greenhouse gas emissions rose slightly, by 0.3%, in the six months after the carbon market took effect. Those opposed to the Carbon Pricing Mechanism decried it as a carbon tax that would harm everyday Australians. Still, only five products saw price increases due to carbon pricing, one of them being electricity, which heavily depends on coal in Australia.

It's not absurd to say the Australian cap-and-trade system was a disaster from the start. The fact that it was met with such partisan resistance meant that they would repeal it as soon as the opposition regained power. Tony Abbott, the leader of the Liberal Party at the time, vowed to "fight this tax every second of every minute of every day" and stated he would repeal the Clean Energy Act if his party won the 2013 election. This uncertainty in government policy made businesses unwilling to invest in major emissions-reduction technology. They had a generally weak response to the cap-and-trade system. The Liberal Party gained power in the 2013 election, and Tony Abbott fulfilled his promise to repeal the Clean Energy Act. When he did so, Australia earned the dubious distinction of being the first country in the world to repeal a carbon pricing system. Today, the nation has a significantly more watered-down carbon pricing program called the Safeguard Mechanism. According to the Climate Action Tracker, Australia is set to miss its climate goals.

Several lessons can be drawn from Australia for other nations interested in carbon pricing policies, but the most obvious is that partisanship can be fatal to emissions trading programs. Bipartisan support is necessary to make a carbon pricing system last regardless of which political party is in power. Organizations will not take a cap-and-trade system seriously if they believe its demise is just around the corner with the next election.

Furthermore, the most common argument against a cap-and-trade program appeared in the Australian battle for carbon pricing: it's a "carbon tax." Tony Abbott called it the "great big tax on everything." The logic behind that argument is that a carbon pricing mechanism would just push up costs for businesses, who would then pass on those costs to customers. One apparent flaw in his claim is that the carbon pricing system affected 0.02% of Australia's businesses. Even if that did result in modest price increases in a small number of goods, it was by no means a tax on "everything."

America and Emissions Trading

Lakes were devastated in parts of North America. The water was so clear that you could see the floor that was fifty feet down. Even the algae that usually blocked light from reaching those depths were gone—the water was entirely lifeless. It was the 20th century, and scientists were confounded as to what was happening. Today, we're well aware that the cause was acid rain, but it took years of experimentation and research for scientists to discover this. It took even longer before serious policy changes to target the cause: sulfur dioxide (SO_2) emissions. There was significant industry pushback to reducing emissions, mirroring the current resistance from energy businesses against the adoption of carbon pricing programs worldwide.

It's not commonly known that the U.S already has a successful emissions trading program. The Acid Rain Program was established as part of the Clean Air Act Amendments in 1990 and exists today. Sulfur dioxide emissions have dropped 40% between the 1990s and the late 2000s. A 2021 study by researchers from UCLA, Columbia, and Cornell found that the "sulfur controls reduced pollution immediately" and that the "Acid Rain Program caused lasting improvements in ambient air quality" and reduced mortality risk by 5% over ten years.

The framework for a successful carbon trading program exists in the European Union Emissions Trading System. The precedent of a national emissions trading system in America does as well. There are even carbon trading systems already in existence among its states. So clearly, the US doesn't lack an emissions trading system from any confusion over its implementation or effectiveness. The issue is, just like Australia, about politics.

Marco Rubio, currently a Republican senator from Florida, stated in a 2010 campaign ad that "If cap-and-trade were imposed on America, it would devastate economic growth, it would get rid of jobs, it would be permanently debilitating." Yet cap-and-trade for sulfur dioxide emissions was a Republican idea. Democrats had been skeptical of the idea initially, not trusting that a market mechanism could fix an environmental issue. According to Robert Stavins, a Harvard economist who was an advisor for the US Environmental Protection Agency under both Republican and Democratic presidents, the change in Republicans' views on cap-and-trade came almost entirely because of a Democratic action in 2009 under the Obama administration. Democrats wanted to pass a climate change bill called the American Clean Energy and Security Act of 2009. The bill would have established an EU ETS-like emissions trading system. Republicans bashed cap-and-trade with the slogan "cap and tax." It worked, and the bill was defeated.

It's clear that one of the biggest challenges to the establishment of new carbon markets is political. That much is obvious to many in these nations. Yet, it's still remarkable just how little these arguments are about achieving what's best for one's nation and rather about winning political battles. Other nations would do well to learn from the mistakes of the US and Australia. The battle to reduce carbon emissions is already herculean, and to let it become a political issue makes the task all the more difficult.

CHAPTER 6

ALTERNATIVE WAYS TO INVEST IN CARBON WITH CARBON-BACKED CRYPTOCURRENCIES

Apart from directly entering the carbon markets or investing in carbon-linked ETFs, a trendy and new way to invest in carbon is to invest in innovative carbon-backed digital assets like cryptocurrencies. As carbon is getting pricier each passing day, many different investors actively put their funds in carbon. As such, innovative blockchain startups have come up with disruptive and innovative means to invest in carbon. Today many different cryptocurrencies are linked to carbon. As such, those who want to invest hassle-free in carbon and enjoy better liquidity can also consider investing in a digital asset like cryptocurrencies that are particularly backed by carbon. The value and price of these digital assets are directly linked to carbon. Therefore, their price reflects the price movement of carbon in the global market.

Carbon Credits and Crypto

Crypto has evolved from the original vision of Satoshi Nakamoto for a digital currency. Today, much of the crypto industry is attempting to build an entire decentralized alternative financial system. One of the fascinating developments in creating this new financial system has been the emergence of unique derivatives and crypto-assets. Among them are projects that tie together cryptocurrencies and Carbon Credits. At first, the combination may seem like another attempt to put anything and everything on a blockchain, whether it makes sense or not. Still, the Carbon Credit market could use some assistance from the foundational technology of cryptocurrencies.

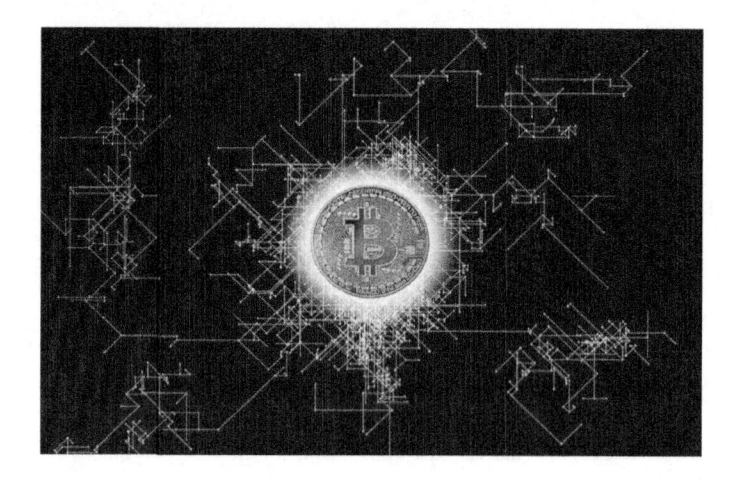

The genius of bitcoin was to create a secure, decentralized digital currency in which double-spending is impossible. And double spending can be a key problem in Carbon Credit markets. Yet, it wasn't until recently that major Carbon Credit crypto projects have taken off. The reason is clear: it's far easier to create a US dollar-backed crypto-asset than a carbon-credit one. Once crypto became a more legitimate industry, business leaders, companies, and nations could launch a serious project.

Early Projects

One of the earlier such projects was AirCarbon, a blockchain-based carbon trading exchange based in Singapore. It launched in 2019, although it took until 2020 to acquire the appropriate licenses from the Monetary Authority of Singapore. AirCarbon isn't particularly well-known within the crypto community because it isn't a platform for retail investors but airlines and other corporations. Its platform allows these clients to trade tokens backed by carbon offset credits that the International Civil Aviation Organization approves. In 2019, the co-founder of AirCarbon claimed that the platform would represent carbon trades with a value above $100 billion. However, there is not much detailed information on its trading volume today because the platform is only for large businesses. Furthermore, the figure of $100 billion seems dubious: in January 2021, the Taskforce on Scaling Voluntary Carbon Markets (TSVCM), sponsored by the Institute of International Finance (IIF), estimated the Carbon Credit market could be worth about $50 billion by 2030.

The move to give retail investors access to Carbon Credits through crypto occurred in December 2020, when the Universal Protocol Alliance announced the Universal Carbon (UPCO2) token launch. The alliance is led by the New York City-based fintech company Uphold and includes the hardware wallet creator Ledger and the crypto exchange company Bittrex Global. The UPCO2 tokens are ERC-20 tokens—in other words, they run on the Ethereum blockchain—and each token represents a certified measure of CO_2. To be more precise, each UPCO2 token represents one year-ton of carbon dioxide emissions prevented by a certified REDD+ project, according to JP Thieriot, the CEO of Uphold and a co-founder of the Universal Protocol Alliance. REDD+ is a framework backed by the United Nations and stands for "Reducing Emissions from Deforestation and forest Degradation." The "+" represents the inclusion of conservation and sustainable management of forests.

The tokens can be bought and sold for investment or speculation, like other crypto assets. Still, they can also be burned to offset the carbon footprint of a company or an individual, according to the alliance. Before UPCO2, retail investors were able to access the market for voluntary Carbon Credits but were unable to hold or trade them, according to Thieriot, who stated in an interview with CoinDesk that, "We are the first people in the world that are making these credits accessible to retail, and holdable."

Corporations like Amazon, Microsoft, and Nike have shown interest in voluntary carbon offsetting, no longer keen on waiting for government action to address the issue of CO_2 emissions, Thieriot said. Regardless of their motivations, whether it's a genuine desire to fight climate change or an interest in making a public relations move to catch the wave of enthusiasm surrounding ESG investing today, this is a positive development that could prove significant in the shift toward reductions of greenhouse gas emissions. UPCO2 tokens began trading on December 1 on Uphold. Bittrex Global listed it on its exchange in February 2021. Of course, even if UPCO2 doesn't take off, a project inspired by it could, in the same way, that bitcoin led to the emergence of Ethereum, which created the DeFi space.

Elon Musk and the MicroStrategy-Tesla Bitcoin Bet

Major players in finance involved themselves in cryptocurrencies before MicroStrategy, but not on the same scale. In August 2020, the company revealed that it had purchased Bitcoin worth US$250 million at the time. It was among the first publicly listed companies in the US to purchase Bitcoin. It followed with an even greater buying-spree of BTC, with its crypto holdings being worth $3.1 billion in February 2021. Eight months after MicroStrategy revealed its Bitcoin position, Tesla purchased huge amounts of BTC worth $1.5 billion in February and announced that customers could purchase its cars with the crypto.

With the significant drop in the price of Bitcoin, their purchases, particularly Tesla's, may not have had the best timing. It remains to be seen whether Bitcoin enters its usual cycle of massive drops and astonishing bull runs, but regardless of the effect of the companies' purchases on their performance, their actions may have been the necessary trigger to greater adoption of cryptocurrencies. In particular, when Elon Musk announced that Tesla would no longer accept Bitcoin for purchases in May 2021, significant attention was brought to the environmental impact of the crypto industry, both from those within and without.

One of the major projects that may benefit from this is Bitcoin Zero, a wrapped ℞C-20 token that involves using the UPCO2 token. A wrapped token is pegged ⁀he value of another crypto asset. The name comes from the fact that the ᵢnal asset is put into a wrapper, which you can think of as a digital piggy that allows the wrapped version to be made on another blockchain. A ₁ Zero token wraps a single real Bitcoin with net-zero emissions. It achieves this by burning ten UPCO2 tokens, which should offset the emissions from Bitcoin production. While the token has yet to gain significant momentum, it could be an attractive investment for corporations interested in Bitcoin without the negative environmental and PR effects of purchasing normal BTC.

Bitcoin has a problem: carbon emissions from mining. While one solution for companies interested in investing in it is simply to switch to a cryptocurrency that isn't as energy-intensive, some projects attempt to fix the problem without such a compromise. The use of Carbon Credit-backed cryptocurrencies could be the solution. Even if Bitcoin mining doesn't reach carbon neutrality rapidly, Carbon Credits could give the crypto assets net-zero emissions regardless. Furthermore, Carbon Credit markets could find significant benefits from blockchain use beyond Bitcoin investment, including a lower risk of double-spending. Finally, Carbon Credit-backed crypto-assets have the potential to change emissions trading if only a major project could be developed that could launch this into prominence and give it the attention necessary for more corporations and governments to research and potentially adopt them.

CHAPTER 7

WHY INVEST IN CARBON

Carbon trade is a multi-billion-dollar market. It is exploding. At present, more than 40 countries and 25 sub-national governments have implemented a price on carbon. Global carbon markets grew by a massive 20% to $272 billion in 2020. In 2019, it reported an unprecedented 34% growth to $225 billion approximately. While the figures are self-explanatory, we all know where we are headed to. It won't be surprising if the global carbon market doubles its size in the next five years. To investors, the carbon market brings a unique and highly profitable opportunity to profit by investing in green and ecological assets. The market size and the prospects are ideal for investors of all shapes and sizes. In this chapter, we will learn about the performance of the carbon markets and understand why it can be a highly profitable venture to invest in carbon.

Profitability and Prospects

The current market standing for Carbon Credits and carbon-linked ETFs suggest that the commodity that is carbon dioxide or GHGs has a long way to go, long enough for your investments in it to grow.

As reported by the Wall Street Journal, in commodities-related investments in 2020, carbon-linked trading funds are among the best performing. This is as the world is putting more effort into combating climate change. Thus, the carbon market and carbon-related investments continue to gain ground and attraction from small and big investors alike.

According to the same report, Carbon Credits in Europe surged 135% over the past year, though still behind lumber. But this is the case given certain conditions that may change over time: tighter government control, weather, inventory gap of liquefied natural gas, among others.

Carbon-related investment funds continue to attract more attention from retail investors and professionals, as noted by a top official of the KraneShares.

One of the world's largest carbon markets, the EU, has expanded by 85% in 2020 from 2017, along with North American carbon makers. As a result, open interest on EU emissions credits also rose to a record-high $105 in May 2020, according to Intercontinental Exchange (ICE).

As the world races to cut down carbon emissions, both the US and EU set respective targets. However ambitious their targets, this race is expected to increase the popularity of the Carbon Credit market and carbon-related ETFs and investments.

China has just recently launched its carbon market, the largest to date. Brussels aims to be "carbon neutral" by 2050.

China's new commitment to seriously combat climate change will steer the global emission trade into a new and exciting phase.

To this date, China is the world's number one contributor of GHG emissions to the atmosphere taking over the place of the United States.

This means that China's carbon market will need more Carbon Credits from its partners to offset their targets and more carbon investment funds to dangle.

Whatever circumstances are considered by those speculating about China's success in reducing its emission, one thing is certain: carbon trading has just become more palatable and offers more profitability.

To guarantee is out of the question. Trading and investment are always learning while doing. But with carbon trading, the future of profit is always bright. The fact alone that China has launched its carbon market is already your signal to start investing now.

There are a total of 137 countries that have pledged to reach net-zero carbon emissions. However, so far, only Bhutan and Suriname were able to achieve carbon neutrality.

Uruguay may be the next to finish the race to net-zero by 2030, followed by countries in Europe: Austria, Finland, Germany, Iceland, and Sweden, whose targets are by 2045 or earlier.

Five other countries have pledged to be carbon neutral after 2050 namely Australia, Singapore, Ukraine, Kazakhstan, and China. The rest of the 124 countries have set a target of 2050.

Most of the industrialized and economies in transition have pledged themselves to this fight against climate change. These countries have also begun to seriously tackle climate change action via emissions trading or the carbon market.

If you place your money now to invest in any of the Carbon Credits-related companies, you might as well find yourself among those you placed their hopes in saving the planet while earning.

The Climate Pledge

Many different companies are pledging funds for mitigating the risks of carbon emissions. One such initiative is the carbon pledge, where signatories are actively pursuing to limit carbon emissions.

Amazon has allocated a dedicated $2 billion Climate Pledge fund to back "sustainable technologies and services" that will, in turn, help Amazon (and other companies) fulfill The Climate Pledge - to be net-zero carbon by 2040

The Climate Pledge is an ongoing call to all businesses and organizations to join a collective climate action. The Pledge signatories confer to working together in facing and taking measures on the planet's greatest crisis. These actions are directed toward building a "safe and healthy" planet for future generations to come.

Co-founded by Amazon and Global Optimism, The Climate Pledge began in

2019 and has since continued to gain more signatories.

The Climate Pledge signatories include Nestle, Ford, Microsoft, Unilever, Coca-Cola, IBM, and Mercedes-Benz.

The Pledge itself is aware that having these signatories would greatly help attract investment in developing low-carbon products and services.

This as it stands on the conviction that these signatories, big businesses themselves, are accountable and responsible. Moreover, they believe that they are capable of acting together to fight the climate crisis.

For an ordinary investor, though, be amazed to earn from as low as a 2-digit US dollar money to as big as your imagination can think of.

Earn these credits from simply planting trees, designing or building renewable, clean energy mechanisms, building your carbon capture technology.

But if you're more of the type who would simply want to invest your money, period, then carbon-linked exchange-traded funds are available for you to explore.

CHAPTER 8

TIPS TO INVESTING IN CARBON

Carbon is increasingly becoming a profitable investment choice for many investors. However, while the carbon-linked ETFs and other assets provide an incredible income opportunity, one always must try to make an informed decision. It is all the more crucial when investing in a market like carbon which is highly diverse and fragmented. In this chapter, we will discuss nine tips to invest smartly in carbon markets.

1. Deciding Your Investment Goals

The first step to becoming a successful investor is to decide your investment goals. While we all want to make some profits with our investments, our investment goals define the nature of the investment. You must decide whether you're investing for a short-term or long-term. How much risk can you take? How important is liquidity for you? You would need to answer many different questions to make sure you are clear with your investment goals. Once you know your particular investment goals, you can start looking for opportunities to accomplish them. Carbon markets are an emerging investment market and provide many different options to help you achieve your investment goals.

2. How Much You Want to Invest

A lot depends on how much you want to invest. The amount you want to invest must be aligned with your investment goals. Also, while deciding how much to invest, you'll have to consider when you need the funds. For example, several carbon-backed ETFs or other similar investment opportunities have a locking period for best returns. To maximize your profitability and not be disappointed, you must make fixed allocations and plan your investments accordingly.

3. How You Choose to Invest in Carbon

Carbon markets are still evolving. They are highly diverse and fragmented, and there are many different ways to start investing in carbon markets. You must choose accordingly. Whether you want to buy Carbon Credits directly from an international carbon market, or you want to invest in Carbon Credit through ETFs, you'll have to make a choice. It is important as all these investments are not the same. Your profitability will depend a lot on how you're investing in carbon. Directly purchasing certificates in the market is one of the most profitable ways, but it is not as quickly processable as an ETF.

4. Selecting the Carbon Markets

When purchasing Carbon Credits or investing in any carbon market across the globe, you must check their credibility and the trade volume. We have already discussed the biggest markets in the chapters above. When investing, it is important to learn more about the carbon markets you want to invest in.

5. Carbon Linked Funds

There are many different Carbon-linked funds. These carbon-linked Exchange-Traded Funds are becoming extremely popular as more and more corporations are pushing to become carbon neutral in the next ten years. Many investors are also putting their money in these funds. However, before purchasing or investing in any Carbon-linked ETF, learning more about what they offer is important. You must track their past performance and know how the fund is invested - how much of the fund is invested in Carbon. The funds with a greater percentage of carbon representation will gain more when the carbon price is up. There are all different kinds of funds with different percentages of carbon representation.

6. Advanced Due Diligence

Regardless of how much you want to invest, it is always recommended that you do advanced due diligence before chipping in. Especially when investing in carbon, you must conduct advanced due diligence on the carbon markets and the exchange trade funds. If you're investing in alternative ways like purchasing digital assets such as cryptocurrencies backed by carbon, it becomes even more important to conduct thorough due diligence. It is important to know how easy it is to encash the funds and bonds you invest in. What are the returns investors have gotten in the past five or ten years? Get to know who manages the fund and how the fund is managed. It is equally important to learn more about what protections you have or how your interests are represented during the entire investment process.

7. Regulatory Compliance

Carbon is an ecological asset, and it is recently gaining popularity. However, there are a lot of regulations, and these are different in different jurisdictions. Investing in any carbon market, it is highly recommended that you first understand the regulations and how they impact your position and the market you're investing in. While most carbon markets allow international players, a professional financial advisor must scrutinize any investment or policy document. It is always recommended to get professional help and understand all regulations and legal implications before investing anything substantial in evolving carbon markets.

8. Carbon-Backed Assets

Investing in carbon-backed assets is becoming increasingly popular, especially amongst younger investors. One of the popular ways to invest in carbon is by buying cryptocurrencies that are backed by carbon. It's relatively easy. And one can directly purchase a cryptocurrency on any cryptocurrency exchange and start trading in carbon. However, you must do your due diligence and inquire into how the currencies are backed by carbon and what protections the creators of these digital assets provide to their investors. Also, never invest in carbon-backed coins that don't have a significant daily trading volume. Avoid investing in any of the carbon-backed cryptocurrency projects that are not listed on a major cryptocurrency exchange. Know the team and those who are behind the carbon-backed cryptocoin you're investing in.

9. Check Liquidity and Locking

The easier it is to get liquidity from your investments, the better investment it is. Therefore, when investing in carbon markets, either directly or by purchasing an exchange-traded fund linked to carbon or buying a cryptocurrency backed by carbon, make sure you choose the option that provides the best liquidity and minimum locking period for your investments. However, in doing so, it is also crucial that you check the best returns the investments can provide while giving the best options to gain liquidity.

Carbon markets are evolving and are one of the fastest-growing investment markets globally. As a result, investing in carbon can be fairly secure and equally profitable. However, like any other investment, there is always a certain element of risk involved. Following these tips, you can make informed investment decisions and become a better investor.

Carbon Trade: The Dawn of a New Age of Investing

CHAPTER 9

WHY WE NEED CARBON TRADE: CARBON EMISSION & ITS IMPACT ON THE ENVIRONMENT

Global warming, climate changes, and carbon emissions have bothered the international scientific community over the last few decades. Global organizations have been actively trying to create awareness on these topics, prompting nations' political leadership to address this concern on a war footing jointly. While everyone is aligned on the seriousness of the situation that threatens our ecosystem today, commercial and political concerns of a short-term nature often result in countries sometimes putting this agenda on the backburner.

As such, taxing carbon is essential. Putting a price on Carbon Credits effectively means charging corporations for carbon emissions in the environment. First, let's understand how carbon and toxic gases impact our environment and why we need to control the emissions.

The sustenance of life and habitability on any planet depends on many factors, one of which is the presence of a life-sustaining atmosphere and relatively moderate temperatures. This has been maintained naturally over the ages on planet Earth, which has helped the evolution of life and the ecosystem around us, as we see it today.

As we are aware, the atmosphere plays a critical role in protecting life on Earth by shielding it from incoming ultraviolet (UV) radiation, keeping the planet warm through insulation, and preventing extremes between day and night temperatures. Earth's atmosphere roughly comprises nitrogen (78%), oxygen

(21%) argon (0.9%). Trace amounts of carbon dioxide, methane, water vapor, and neon compromise the other remaining .01%. But this proportion has been changing over time. Once primarily composed of carbon dioxide (arising from volcanic eruptions) and methane (produced by early microbes), the evolution of photosynthetic organisms led to an increase in oxygen in the atmosphere.

But how does the atmosphere manage to moderate temperatures? Temperatures on the earth's surface, air, and oceans are managed through the "Greenhouse effect."

Greenhouse effect: The greenhouse effect is the natural process of setting the Earth's temperature. Some part of the Sun's energy rebounding from the earth's surface is absorbed by greenhouse gases and re-radiated to create a warming effect within the atmosphere. The Earth's temperature depends on the balance between the incoming and outgoing energy levels. Any disruption in this balance leads to an increase or decrease in the surface temperature and causes fluctuations in the atmospheric, oceanic, and land temperatures.

Elements that play a role in managing this effect are called greenhouse gases. These gases are capable of absorbing ultraviolet radiation from the Sun. Various gases contribute to the greenhouse effect. Water vapor, carbon dioxide, methane, nitrous oxide, ozone, and artificial chemicals such as chlorofluorocarbons (CFCs) comprise greenhouse gases.

Due to the potential and efficiency of each gas to absorb and radiate heat, minor changes in the composition of these gases may very well determine whether there is an ice age playing out on the surface of the planet or extreme heat where only the dinosaurs can survive.

Greenhouse effect

1. Solar energy

GREENHOUSE GASES

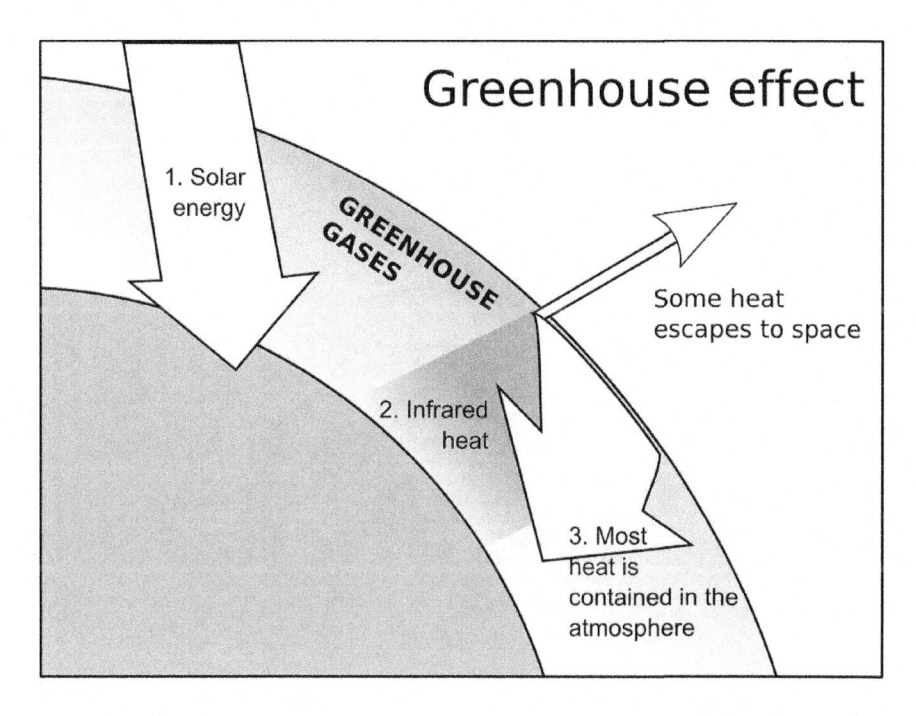

Some heat escapes to space

2. Infrared heat

3. Most heat is contained in the atmosphere

Two factors influence the potency of a greenhouse gas to influence warming. Their ability to absorb energy and radiate it, and second the time it stays potent before it decays or converts through a natural chemical process. A gas with a longer lifetime and higher concentration in the atmosphere may cause a higher increase in the surface temperature despite a lower radiation efficiency than a more potent gas, which is present in the atmosphere over a shorter duration or in lesser concentration in the atmosphere.

You may ask why greenhouse gases are now a cause for concern, especially since they have been in the atmosphere for millions of years.

There are both natural and human sources of carbon emissions. Natural carbon emission sources include ocean-atmosphere exchange, plant and animal respiration, soil respiration and decomposition, volcanic eruptions. These sources have always existed but were naturally neutralized as a similar amount got depleted(sinks) through photosynthesis and soil and ocean absorption.

However, humans upset this equilibrium when they introduced new sources of emission. Greenhouse gases, including the carbon-containing gases carbon dioxide and methane, are emitted through the burning of fossil fuels, land clearance, and the production and consumption of food, manufactured goods, materials, wood, roads, buildings, transportation, and other services.

Since 1800, the global population has grown from 1 billion to 7.9 billion in 2020. The United Nations projections are expected to touch the 11 billion mark by the turn of the century. To manage the needs of this ever-multiplying population, humans have been ravaging nature by cutting down forests (depleting "sinks"), bringing in more areas under cultivation, increasing levels of livestock, etc. In turn, this increasing population has been drying up water resources, generating sewage, and polluting the environment by its sheer footfall. On the one hand, humans have been ravaging nature. On the other hand is "Industrialization," a process that started in the 18th century and has caused irreversible damage to the environment due to the high levels of pollution it has been causing through extensive use of fossil fuels.

The following table illustrates the increase in the concentration of some greenhouse gases due to industrialization and the Global Warming Potential of each of these gases due to their ability to absorb heat. This potency of individual gases to impact global warming is defined as the 'Global Warming Potential'(GWP), a measure of the radiative effect of each unit of gas by weight over a specific period of time, expressed relative to the radiative effect of carbon dioxide. Gases with higher GWP will warm the earth more than an equal amount of CO2. However, as seen from the table, CO2 significantly impacts global warming with its sheer volume and concentration. About half of cumulative anthropogenic CO2 emissions between the years 1750 and 2010 have occurred since 1970.

Table-1

Name of the Gas	Global Warming Potential	Atmospheric Lifetime in Years	Pre Industrial Concentration (ppb)	2011 Concentration (ppb)
Carbon Dioxide	1	100	278K	390K
Methane	25	12	722	1803
Nitrous Oxide	265	121	271	324
CFC-12	10200	100	nil	0,527
HFC - 23	12400	222	nil	0.024

Source: *Fifth Assessment Report (Intergovernmental Panel on Climate Change 2014)*
PPB: *Parts per billion.*

The burning of fossil fuels is estimated to contribute more than 62% of the human carbon emissions, 12% of total emissions arise from agriculture, 7% from land-use change and forestry, 6% from industrial processes, and 3% from waste. Around 6% of emissions are fugitive emissions, which are waste gases released by extracting fossil fuels.

Carbon footprints: Efforts have been on since the 1990s to measure the amount of carbon emission caused by a single activity. A '**Carbon footprint**' is the total greenhouse gas (GHG) emissions caused by an individual, event, organization, service, place, or product, expressed as carbon dioxide equivalent. The following method of measuring the carbon footprint was proposed by William E. Rees and Mathis Wackernagel in the 1990s:

A measure of the total amount of carbon dioxide (CO2) and methane (CH4) emissions of a defined population, system or activity, considering all relevant sources, sinks and storage within the spatial and temporal boundary of the population, system or activity of interest. Calculated as carbon dioxide equivalent using the relevant 100-year global warming potential (GWP100).

Greenhouse effect impact: The increase in the greenhouse gases, and consequently an enhanced greenhouse effect, has been identified to have had long-term heating of the Earth's climate system. As a result, the earth's global average temperature is estimated to have increased by 1 degree Celsius and constantly increasing by 0.2 degrees per decade.

A. Global Warming directly influences weather and climate patterns and has caused large-scale changes in climatic patterns.
B. Ice cores were drawn from Greenland, Antarctica, and tropical mountain glaciers show that Earth's climate responds to changes in greenhouse gas levels. Ancient evidence can also be found in tree rings, ocean sediments, coral reefs, and layers of sedimentary rocks. This ancient, or paleoclimate, evidence reveals that current warming is occurring roughly ten times faster than the average rate of ice-age-recovery warming.
C. Air temperatures have increased globally by around 1.18 degrees Celsius since the last century, with most changes occurring after 1970. This results in a decrease in the colder-than-average days and an increase in warmer-than-average days reported across regions. As a result, 2016 and 2020 have recorded the warmest temperatures in recorded history.
D. Oceans are the largest repository of atmospheric heat, and more than 90% of the heat generated by the added greenhouse impact is absorbed by the oceans. Ocean warming is continuing, especially in the top several hundred meters of the ocean. Studies have shown that the deepest ocean water in the Antarctic, usually the coldest water, has warmed and become less saline since the 1980s. The world's deep ocean currents play a critical role in transporting heat around the planet, thus regulating the climate. The warming of these currents alters their ability to perform this function.
E. Acidification of the oceans increases with the increasing concentration of

carbon dioxide in the atmosphere, which gets dissolved in the oceans forming carbonic acid.

F. Marine life and ecosystems get impacted by this acidification. Increasing acidification and even minor increases in average temperatures destroy marine plants, corals, and other invertebrates as they cannot evolve faster to keep pace with the temperature increases. Moreover, organisms that form shells or bodies of calcium carbonate are unable to precipitate the minerals. While these changes are likely to have the greatest impacts on marine environments such as coral reefs and the Arctic and Antarctic ecosystems, it's only a matter of time before all aquatic ecosystems are affected by increasing ocean warming and acidification levels.

G. The Greenland and Antarctic ice sheets have decreased in mass due to higher average temperatures. Data from NASA's Gravity Recovery and Climate Experiment show Greenland lost an average of 279 billion tons of ice per year between 1993 and 2019, while Antarctica lost about 148 billion tons of ice per year. Likewise, glaciers across the Himalayas, Alps, Andes & Alaska are retreating due to rapid melting. This directly increases the sea levels and leads to submerging of low-level areas on the shores. Global sea level rose about eight inches (twenty centimeters) in the last century. However, the rate in the last two decades is nearly double that of the last century and accelerating slightly every year. Increasing surrender of land to the oceans will disrupt millions of communities living along the shores.

H. Extreme weather and climate events have serious impacts on our economy, society, and environment. Extreme weather events include heatwaves, bushfires, tropical cyclones, cold snaps, extreme rainfall, including flash flooding and droughts. These are triggered by disruption in the climate patterns and increased temperatures.

I. Wet areas are likely to get wetter and dry regions are likely to be drier in response to climate change. This also results in changes in the growing season and disruption of crop patterns. The disruption to food production due to these changes will directly impact the ever-growing food requirements of the human population. Every year millions of people worldwide suffer from hunger and food insecurity. Climate change and increased drought, pests, and other climate-related side effects threaten to further impact every facet of food production, from food quality to people's ability to access it.

The above changes do not cover the socio-economic impact of the above large-scale changes and how they might impact future generations.

Mitigation: Responding to climate change involves two possible approaches: reducing and stabilizing the levels of greenhouse gases and/or adapting to the climate change already in the pipeline. Since the impact of the greenhouse gases already in the atmosphere will persist for a long time, we have to be prepared for the impending climate changes.

Reducing climate change involves reducing the flow of greenhouse gases into the atmosphere by reducing these gases or increasing the "sinks" that help absorb these gases. The idea is to avoid significant human interference with the climatic system. Moreover, even stabilizing such gases will help the ecosystem adapt naturally to climate change.

The United Nations Framework Convention on Climate Change, which came into effect in 1994, and its "Kyoto Protocol" that came into effect in 2005: sharing the objective of the Convention to stabilize atmospheric concentrations of greenhouse gases. The protocol sets binding targets for developed countries (the signatories) to limit or reduce greenhouse gas emissions apart from creating a framework for implementing an array of national policies.

The protocol also stimulated the creation of a Carbon market. Targets Assigned to nations are denominated in individual units called Assigned Amount Units (AAU), each of which represents an allowance to emit one tonne of CO_2 equivalent termed as Carbon Credits. These are then monitored through a national registry. Individual units are then allocated to businesses and organizations based on their carbon footprint. These units are tradable. Accordingly, institutions that can save on their allocations, i.e., generate fewer emissions than the allocated units, can sell these credits in the open market. Therefore, the incentive to save acts as a trigger for the collective achievement of the global emission reduction targets.

The increase in carbon emission impacts us by threatening our whole ecosystem. Humans have woken up to this threat, albeit slowly. However, aggressive measures are needed to stop further deterioration. Both awareness levels and participation by everyone are the keys to sustaining the baby steps taken as we seek a secure future in our ecosystem.

Carbon Trade: The Dawn of a New Age of Investing

CONCLUSION

PROS AND CONS OF INVESTING IN CARBON MARKETS

The world is battling climate change and cutting down carbon emissions is quintessential to the planet's future. As an investor, there are many things one must consider. Carbon is a sustainable and green investment that also brings profits. There are many advantages, but a few critics of carbon markets have been calling it ineffective. However, let's take a look at the advantages and disadvantages of investing in Carbon markets.

Pros of Investing in Carbon Markets:

1. By Investing in Carbon, You Also Invest in the Future of the Planet

The very idea of taxing and putting a price on carbon aims to limit the emission of toxic gases. With a price on carbon emission, the industries and factories have to pay for pumping toxic gases into the environment. Carbon trade and the introduction of Carbon Credits have helped in putting a check on indiscriminate carbon pumping. Investing in carbon makes you a responsible investor.

2. Global Market

Carbon Credit is a global ecological asset, and you have multiple options to choose from. Depending on your ability to invest, you can also move to overseas markets. Almost all major economies have a carbon market, and there are plenty of opportunities. For example, recently, China launched its first and the world's biggest carbon markets. It also offers competent investment schemes for players in the Carbon trade.

3. One of the Most Profitable Asset Classes

Carbon has emerged as one of the most profitable asset classes in recent years. The EU ETS Carbon Credit Futures, one of the most prominent, has gained as much as 574% since 2018. With the Paris Agreement on climate change, most countries are aiming to become carbon neutral by 2050. That means the market would be worth over 100 billion in the US alone. The profits are likely to increase because of the growing pressure. To reduce carbon emissions, the prices of the Carbon Credits or the permits to pump carbon into the environment must be higher. It's only when carbon pumping factories owned by big corporations will have to pay more that they will be responsible for their carbon emissions. As such, in the near future, we will only see carbon prices getting higher and higher.

4. The Market Size

With more and more businesses shifting their focus to limiting carbon emissions, Carbon Credits have emerged as one of the fastest-growing ecological assets. The market in the US alone is about $24 billion representing about 12% of the world's carbon market. Article 6 of the UNFCCC Paris Agreement calls for the prices of Carbon credit to be doubled from between $100/tCO2 by 2030.

"Carbon markets grew 5x in the last 3 years to a record high of $215B in 2019. The market size in the USA jumped 74% to $24B & China up 40% to $300M."

The UN estimates that the carbon markets globally have the potential to generate $26 trillion in growth.

5. Multiple Options to Invest in Carbon

If you're new to investing in ecological assets, it may be overwhelming. However, now that you have learned about the carbon markets, you must be confident about the opportunities. There are many different ways and options to invest in carbon. For example, you can invest in Carbon Credits at the world's biggest carbon markets. You can choose to invest in carbon-backed bonds. You can invest in carbon offset ETFs. Or you can also choose to invest in cryptocurrencies that are backed by Carbon Credits. The range of choices allows you to benefit from the best opportunity and gives you the flexibility to enter the market regardless of the size of your investment.

6. Carbon Neutrality is Corporate Goal of Industry Leaders

Most of the bigger corporations are pushing toward carbon neutrality by 2030. With the awareness about climate change and carbon growing, it is important for their business and branding as much as it is for the environment. With top companies trying to become carbon neutral, they will need to purchase Carbon Credits. It is impossible for businesses to simply minimize their carbon emissions. However, they will have to purchase Carbon Credits which again will drive both demand and price of carbon assets and funds. For example, Amazon has set a $10 billion climate fund. It is aiming to become carbon neutral by 2040. The tech giant Microsoft corporation is claiming to become carbon neutral by 2030. It also has a $1 billion climate fund. The list of corporations planning carbon neutrality is long.

While there are many promising advantages of investing in carbon, there are a few concerns as well. However, these concerns don't qualify as a disadvantage as such.

- A. **Critics Of Carbon Credit Say There Should Be No Carbon Markets:** While Carbon trade and taxing, and pricing carbon has proven to help reduce carbon emissions, critics say that there should be no price on carbon. Their argument is by pricing carbon. We still allow corporations to pump carbon into the environment. The problem is practically, it is not possible for corporations and factories to neutralize their carbon emissions. As such, by putting a price on carbon, countries can incentivize decreasing carbon emissions. Also, the best way to make these factories limit their carbon pumping to a minimum is by increasing the price of Carbon Credits.

B. **Lack Of Awareness:** The carbon trade is evolving. Generally, investors are not very well aware of the opportunities in the market. Also, the market is highly diversified, and it's not easy to pick an entry route to invest in. However, recently, many carbon-linked funds and bonds have allowed even newbies and retail investors to invest in Carbon Credits. As the market expands and carbon trading becomes more and more popular, investors will have more opportunities. We are already witnessing digital assets backed by carbon becoming increasingly popular lately.

This book is only for informational purposes, and it does not offer financial advice. Readers are requested to take professional financial advice from certified and practicing financial experts before making any investment-related decision. Also, one must understand that cryptocurrency investments are subject to market risks. Therefore, expert due diligence is recommended before investing.

Carbon Trade: The Dawn of a New Age of Investing

Printed in Great Britain
by Amazon